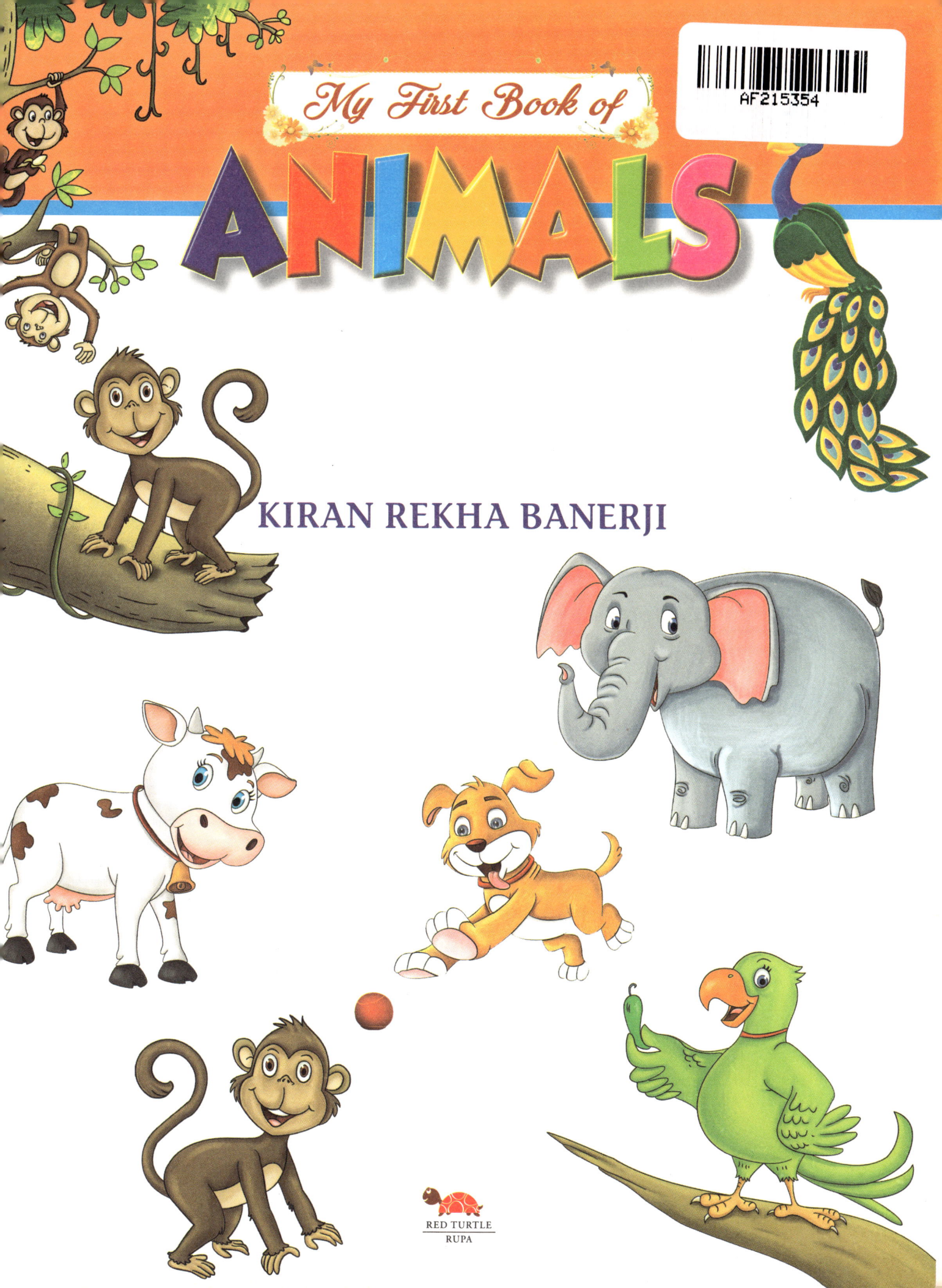

My First Book of ANIMALS

KIRAN REKHA BANERJI

RED TURTLE
RUPA

Published in Red Turtle by
Rupa Publications India Pvt. Ltd 2017
7/16, Ansari Road, Daryaganj
New Delhi 110002

Sales centres:
Allahabad Bengaluru Chennai
Hyderabad Jaipur Kathmandu
Kolkata Mumbai

Text Copyright © Kiran Rekha Banerji 2017
Illustrations Copyright © Rupa Publications India Pvt. Ltd 2017
Design by Roy Creation

The views and opinions expressed in this book are the author's own and the facts are as reported by him/her which have been verified to the extent possible, and the publishers are not in any way liable for the same.

ISBN: 978-81-291-4554-3

First impression 2017

10 9 8 7 6 5 4 3 2 1

The moral right of the author has been asserted.

Printed at Shree Maitrey Printech Pvt. Ltd, Noida

This book belongs to:

....

....

DOMESTIC ANIMALS

Dog

I am Shaggy the dog. I am friendly and love people. I love to eat meat, cereals, biscuits and drink milk. I wag my tail when I am happy. I bark at strangers to keep you safe. My babies are called puppies. They are very playful.

Cat

I am Fuzzy the cat, with soft and fluffy fur. I like to curl up on a bed. My shiny eyes can see even in the dark! I like to drink milk and eat fish. I mew when I am hungry. My babies are called kittens. They love to run around and hide. Oh my! One of my four kittens is hiding! Can you find it?

Cow

I am Moo-moo the cow. I say 'moo' in a deep voice. I live on a farm and eat grass, hay, vegetables and corn. I give milk that makes you grow strong. My milk is also used to make butter, ghee and cheese. My baby is called a calf.

Goat

I am Billy the goat. I like to eat grass and vegetables. I also munch on bread and cereals. I live on a farm. My milk is made into cheese. My baby is called a kid. Kids are playful and skip all around the farm. I say 'baa-baa' when I bleat. Can you find my six kids on the farm?

Horse

I am Trotty the horse. I live in a stable. I eat plenty of fresh grass, hay and grains. I need lots of space to run about. Sometimes I take children for a ride on my back. My baby is called a foal. It likes to trot beside me. I neigh when I am hungry.

Duck

I am Diggy the duck. I live on a farm. I love to swim in the pond with my babies. My baby is called a duckling. I dive into the water to catch small fish for food. I also eat grains and weeds. I say 'quack quack' to call my brood of ducklings. My ducklings love to swim too. Can you see what they have found in the water?

Hen

I am Pecky the hen. I lay eggs that you eat to grow strong. I eat lots of grain, small worms and insects. I live in a hencoop with other hens. I wake up very early in the morning. My babies are called chicks. They follow me everywhere. Can you count all the chicks in the picture?

WILD ANIMALS

Lion

I am Gruffy the lion. I live in the jungle. I am called the king of the jungle. I have thick fur around my neck called mane. I live with my family in a den. My family is called a pride. I hunt animals for food. My loud roar can be heard from far away. My babies are called cubs. Can you count my cubs?

Elephant

I am Tun-tun the elephant. I am the largest animal on land. I have a long trunk that helps me to eat, drink, and even wash myself. I can lift heavy objects with my trunk too! I eat leaves, grass and fruits but bananas are my favourite food. I live in a large family called a herd. Papa elephant has long white teeth called tusks. Can you find papa elephant in the herd?

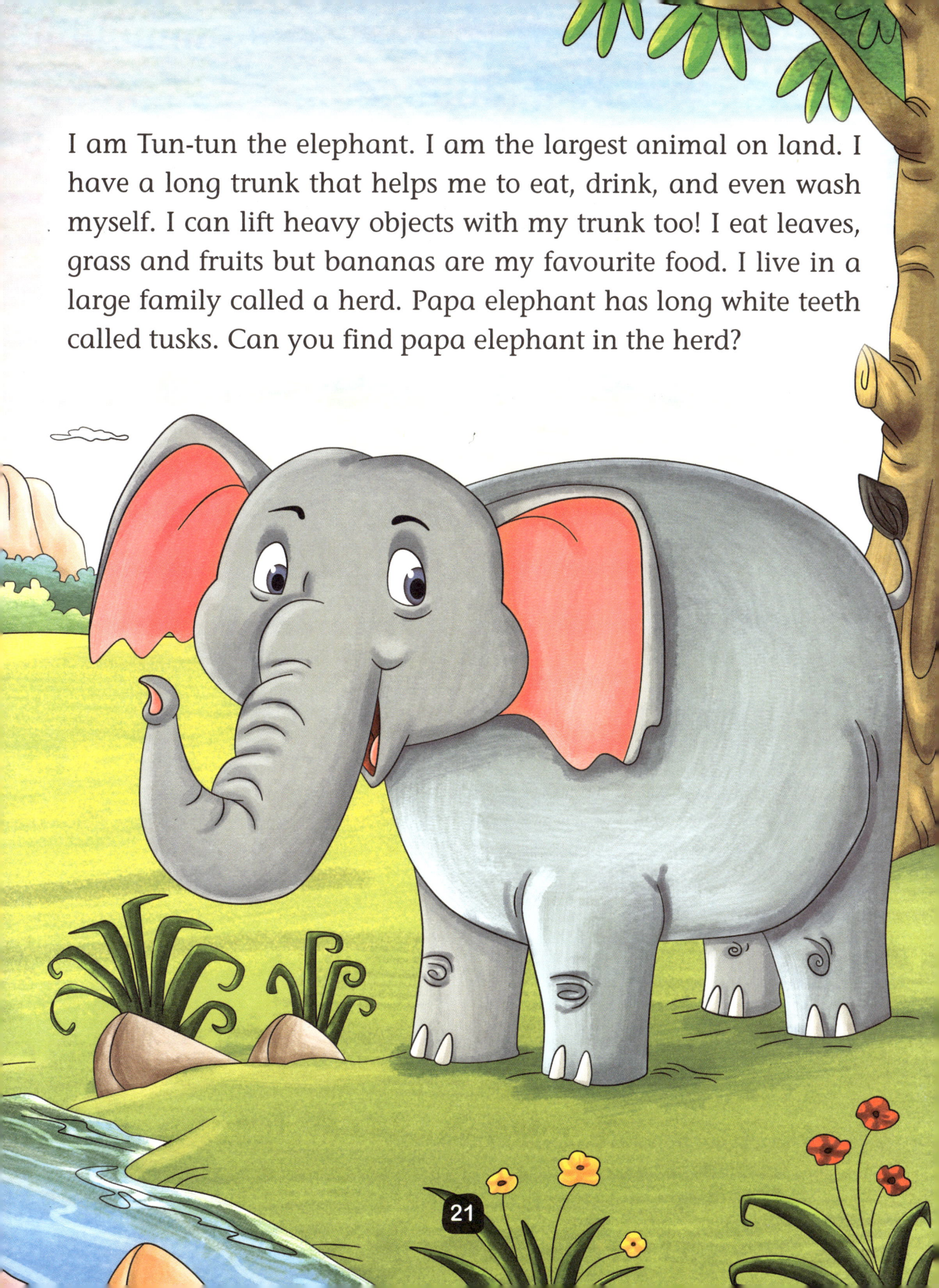

Tiger

I am Stripy the tiger. My striped body makes me look handsome. It also helps me to hide in the jungle where I live. No two tigers have the same pattern of stripes. I am a very good swimmer. I can climb on trees too. I can also run very fast. I have a deep growl that frightens everyone. Can you think of one more animal that has stripes?

Monkey

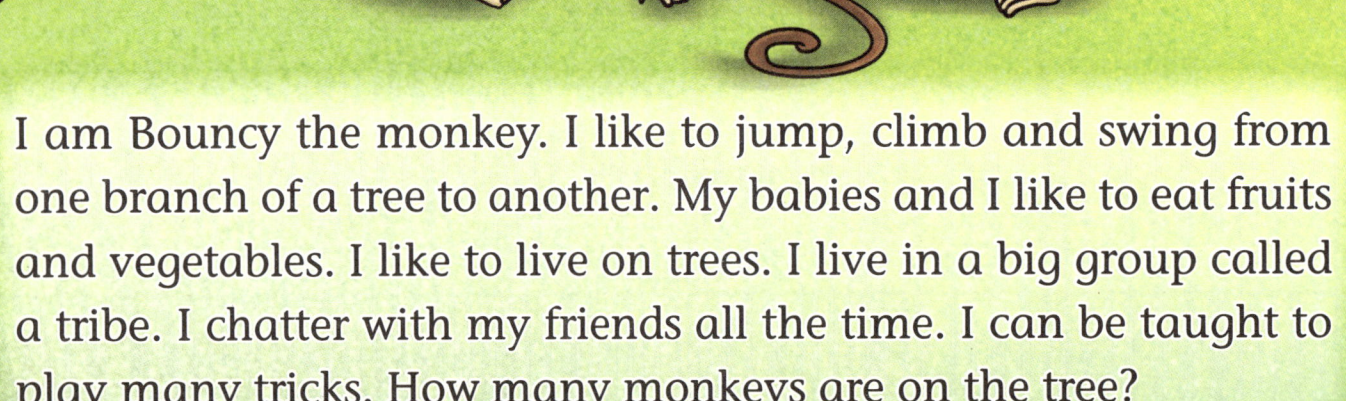

I am Bouncy the monkey. I like to jump, climb and swing from one branch of a tree to another. My babies and I like to eat fruits and vegetables. I like to live on trees. I live in a big group called a tribe. I chatter with my friends all the time. I can be taught to play many tricks. How many monkeys are on the tree?

BIRDS

Parrot

I am Poly the parrot. I can easily hide myself in trees because of my bright green colour. I have a curved, red beak. I can learn to speak words if I am kept as a pet. I like to eat hard and raw fruits but green chillies are my favourite. How many parrots are sitting on branches?

Peacock

I am Cheeku the peacock. I have a long, colourful tail with designs that look like eyes. I am the most beautiful bird in the world! When it is cloudy, I open up my tail feathers like a large fan. I can fly for a short distance only. I have a sharp loud call. Do you know that some people collect my tail feathers?

Pigeon

I am Titu the pigeon. I coo all the time. Some of my cousins are white and brown. We fly in groups in search of grains. We can make a nest and lay eggs almost anywhere! We are also kept as pets. Do you know that in old times pigeons were trained to carry letters? Can you count the eggs in my nest?

Match the animals with their call.

chatter

roar

moo

neigh

coo

bark